FEARS AND FACTS

PATRICIA NEWMAN

M MILLBROOK PRESS / MINNEAPOLIS

With love for Megan and Mia —P.N.

Special thanks to two health-care experts in the field who guided me during the research and writing process: Karlyn D. Beer, MS, Ph.D., Epidemic Intelligence Service Officer, Centers for Disease Control and Prevention, who shared her experience in Liberia and who said, "The reason I'm doing the job I am is because I read a book like this," and Julie Wardinsky, RN, BSN, CIC and Infection Preventionist with Dignity Health for sharing her experience in talking to children about serious diseases.

Millbrook Press
A division of Lerner Publishing Group, Inc.
241 First Avenue North
Minneapolis, MN 55401 USA

Main body text set in Univers LT Std 12/18
Typeface provided by Adobe Systems.

For reading levels and more information, look up this title at www.lernerbooks.com.

Library of Congress Cataloging-in-Publication Data

Newman, Patricia, 1958- author.
  Ebola : fears and facts / by Patricia Newman.
       pages cm
    Summary: "What's Ebola? Do we need to be afraid? This short book will take readers beyond the headlines to help them understand the 2014 outbreak. It will inform while helping to alleviate fears."—Provided by publisher.
    Audience: Ages 9–14
    Audience: Grades 4 to 6
    ISBN 978-1-4677-9240-0 (lb : alk. paper)
    ISBN 978-1-4677-9259-2 (eb pdf)
    1. Ebola virus disease—Juvenile literature. 2. Hemorrhagic diseases—Juvenile literature.
    3. Epidemics—Juvenile literature. I. Title.
RC140.5.N49 2016
616.9'1—dc23   2015001167

Manufactured in the United States of America
1 – PC – 7/15/15

CONTENTS

INTRODUCTION : THE BLACK RIVER — 5

CHAPTER ONE : THE EBOLA PUZZLE — 9

CHAPTER TWO : THE 2014 HOT ZONE — 17

CHAPTER THREE : ON THE FRONT LINES — 29

CHAPTER FOUR : CONQUERING EBOLA — 37

Frequently Asked Questions about Ebola — 42

Author's Note — 44

Glossary — 44

Source Notes — 45

Selected Bibliography — 46

Further Reading — 47

Index — 48

These huts form part of a fishing village that sits on the banks of the Congo River. Part of this river flows into the Ebola River in the Democratic Republic of the Congo.

THE BLACK RIVER

EBOLA. The word calls up images of sick people in Africa and doctors wearing space-suit-like protective gear. Before 1976, however, Ebola was simply the name of a winding river in central Africa. The local people drink its water, eat its fish, and travel its currents. Crops grow in the rich red earth along its banks.

A dense rain forest borders the river's twisting path. The air is thick and damp. Giant trees soar 100 feet (30 meters) in the air and form a canopy that blocks most of the sunlight. Overhead, monkeys hoot. A leopard snoozes on a wide tree limb, while rodents scurry along the forest floor. The air hums and buzzes with billions of insects and frogs. A slurry of mud covers the ground in the rainy season.

Outside this forest sits the village of Yambuku in the Democratic Republic of the Congo (formerly Zaire). The headmaster of the mission school there returned from a trip to the northern part of the country the first week in September 1976. He became ill and died. A few days after his funeral, the nuns who cared for the headmaster, his wife, and other unrelated people became ill. They all suffered from high

The hospital at the Yambuku mission recorded the first known cases of Ebola. This photo was taken in 1976, at the time of the first outbreak.

A team of scientists, including Peter Piot *(second from left)* arrived in Yambuku in October 1976 to investigate a new deadly disease.

fevers, uncontrollable vomiting, bloody diarrhea, and severe nosebleeds. Dr. Jacques Courteille, from the capital city of Kinshasa, treated some of the nuns and a priest from Yambuku. At first, he suspected yellow fever, but yellow fever patients do not bleed like these patients did. He sent samples of one nun's blood to a Belgian laboratory for testing. Scientists ruled out yellow fever and Lassa fever, another bloody illness. No one in the lab had ever seen this disease before.

A team of scientists from around the world traveled to Yambuku to gather more information. Pilots agreed to fly to the village only if they could leave the minute the scientists had unloaded their gear. News of the mysterious sickness reached other villages, and people were frightened. When the plane carrying the scientists arrived, local residents surrounded it. The last plane had landed several weeks earlier, and the villagers were desperate for food and supplies. When they realized the plane carried only scientists, they pressed forward hoping to board it to escape the terrifying disease. Others barricaded the entrances of their villages against strangers to protect themselves. More than one hundred people had died of the disease, including nine out of seventeen hospital staff, thirty-nine people who lived at the mission, four nuns, and two priests. Scientists used detective work to trace the path of the disease and find those who had been exposed. They isolated the sick to limit the spread.

One evening after an exhausting day of work, the scientists suggested names for this deadly new illness. They studied a map of Zaire. "It looked

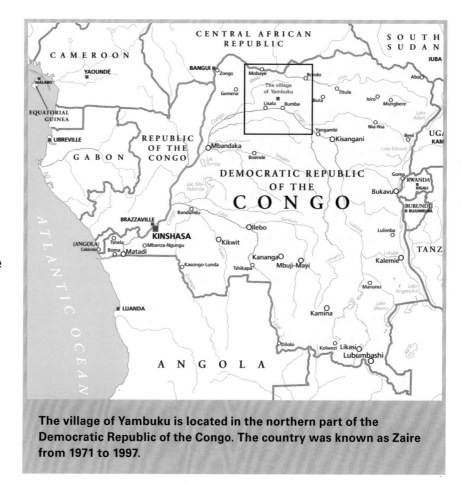

The village of Yambuku is located in the northern part of the Democratic Republic of the Congo. The country was known as Zaire from 1971 to 1997.

as though the closest river to Yambuku was called Ebola—'Black River,' in Lingala. It seemed suitably ominous," said Peter Piot, one of the scientists who discovered the disease. "Actually there's no connection between the hemorrhagic fever and the Ebola River. Indeed, the Ebola River isn't even the closest river to the Yambuku mission. But in our entirely fatigued state, that's what we ended up calling [the disease]."

Ever since the first outbreak ended, Ebola has reappeared in central Africa without warning. Sometimes one, three, or up to fifteen years have passed between outbreaks. But one thing is clear: if scientists want to defeat Ebola once and for all, they need to understand it.

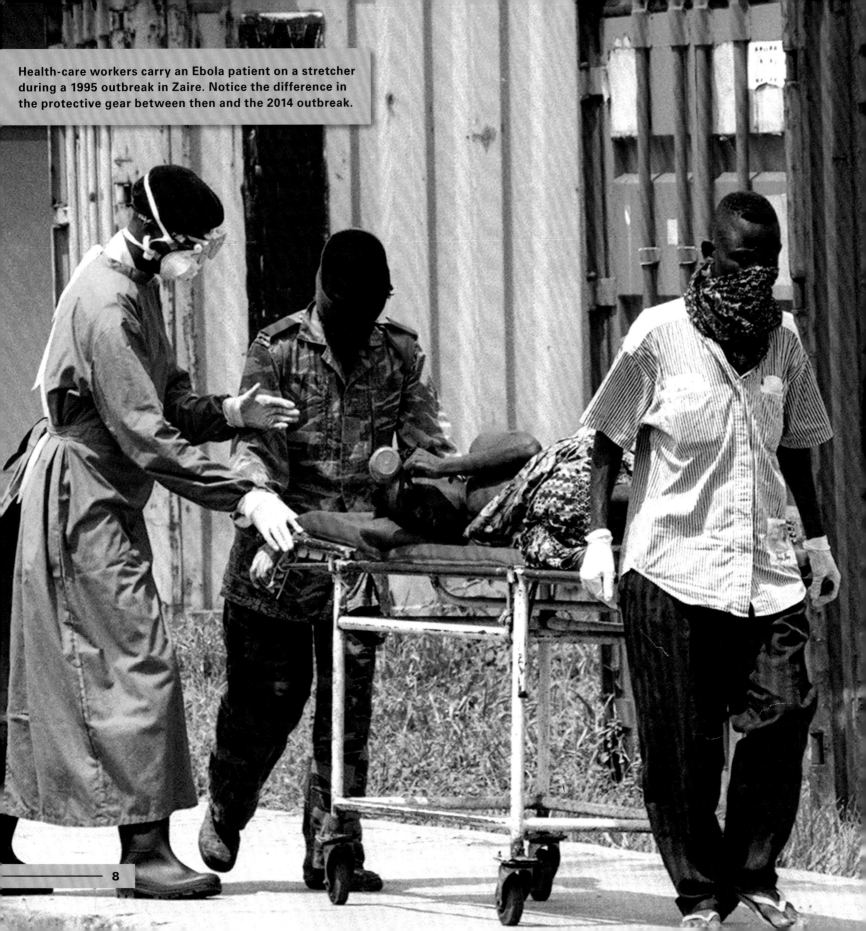

Health-care workers carry an Ebola patient on a stretcher during a 1995 outbreak in Zaire. Notice the difference in the protective gear between then and the 2014 outbreak.

CHAPTER ONE

THE EBOLA PUZZLE

Between 1976 and 1996, central Africa experienced five Ebola outbreaks. Scientists began to notice patterns in Ebola symptoms and how the disease is transmitted. Ebola seems to reappear after villagers somehow disturb the jungle, such as hunting or clearing brush. In roughly two to twenty-one days after this contact, patients develop a fever, muscle aches, a sore throat, and a headache. As Ebola progresses, patients experience intense pain and uncontrollable vomiting and bloody diarrhea. They may also bleed from their eyes or gums. People near death may bleed from their ears, nose, and rectum. Ebola kills quickly because it overwhelms the immune system and basically tricks the body into surrendering. On average, half of all Ebola patients die. In some outbreaks, the disease kills 25 percent of the people who become ill, but in others it kills as many as 90 percent. Scientists noticed that after the first person fell ill in each outbreak, the spread of the disease seemed to be connected to funerals for the victims.

The 1996 outbreak illustrates these patterns perfectly. A group of boys from a remote village in northern Gabon entered the jungle to hunt for bushmeat

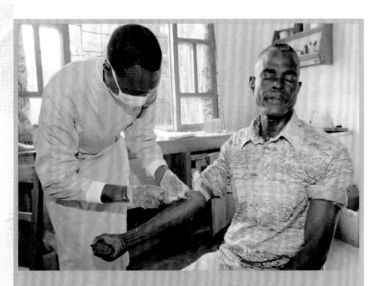

A nurse draws blood from a man who has been in contact with a person who died from Ebola.

In 1995 residents of Kikwit, Zaire, cover their faces to protect themselves against the Ebola virus. They did not understand that Ebola is not an airborne virus and that droplets of blood, vomit, or feces can still infect people through their skin and hands.

to feed their families. They came across a chimpanzee carcass lying on the forest floor and took it home. The eighteen people who ate the meat became sick with fevers, muscle aches, sore throats, and headaches. In a few more days, patients vomited and developed bloody diarrhea. Then Ebola weakened their blood vessels, and blood leaked from their eyes and gums.

Family members tried to nurse the sick, but they didn't have protective gear, so they too became ill. When they scratched their noses, rubbed their eyes, or paused to eat lunch, the sweat, saliva, blood, vomit, or feces from the sick infected them. More relatives came to help, and the virus spread from person to person. Thirty-one villagers became ill with Ebola during the 1996 Gabon outbreak, and twenty (nearly two-thirds) of them died.

A person with Ebola is still contagious after death. Family and friends don't want to bury a loved one covered in blood, feces, or vomit, so they wash the body. Sadly, this practice results in further spread of the disease.

One of the reasons Ebola frightens people is because it currently has no cure.

Like the common cold, we have to wait for it to run its course. Potential vaccines and treatments are only in the testing phase and aren't widely available. In the hospital, doctors and nurses focus on easing patients' symptoms. Clean drinking water and electrolytes reduce dehydration from vomiting and diarrhea. Pain medication helps make patients more comfortable. Other medicines help stop vomiting.

Approximately half of the patients who contract Ebola survive. The survivors' immune systems make antibodies that defeat the virus. These same antibodies also make them immune to future infection. Some scientists believe their immunity could last ten years or longer, but more research is necessary.

When scientists first saw the structure of Ebola under an electron microscope in 1976, they knew it was a virus. Viruses cause many illnesses—from the common cold to influenza to measles. They are microscopic oddballs, neither alive nor dead. They don't eat or drink. They cannot reproduce by themselves. They don't need oxygen

How Ebola Affects the Human Body

Early Stages

headache
sore throat
muscle pain
fever
fatigue

Advanced Stages

bleeding from eyes, nose, and mouth
vomiting
rash
impaired liver and kidneys
diarrhea
internal and external bleeding

A person exposed to Ebola may take up to twenty-one days to develop symptoms. During the 2014 outbreak, the virus killed about two-thirds of those who tested positive for it.

to survive. Until they find the right environment, they exist in a zombielike state. Unfortunately for us, the Ebola virus seems to thrive best in humans and apes.

Ebola looks like a worm. Tiny spikes along its surface act like Velcro and attach to another organism's cells so the virus can invade like an enemy army. Once inside its host, the virus does what viruses are programmed to do—replicate as fast as possible. Ebola first targets several kinds of immune cells that are usually the first line of defense in fighting a disease. It also blocks a molecule called interferon used to halt the replication of viruses. The virus damages so many cells so quickly that they can no longer make the proteins that clot blood. Patients hemorrhage, or bleed. They often die of dehydration, low blood pressure, shock, or organ failure.

But where did the Ebola virus come from? At least one of the millions of species that live in the African rain forest acts as an Ebola reservoir. This animal carries the virus in its body without suffering any ill effects. This creature goes about its business, all the while having the ability to spread the virus. Perhaps a chimpanzee eats a plant

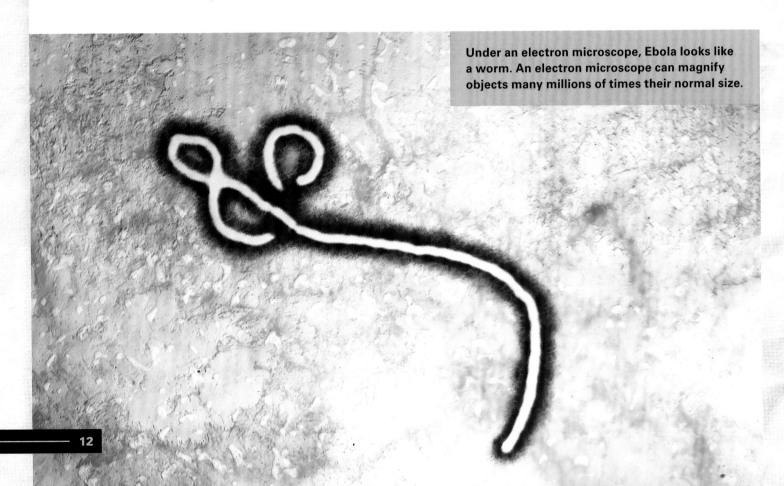

Under an electron microscope, Ebola looks like a worm. An electron microscope can magnify objects many millions of times their normal size.

The flying fox bat is one species of fruit bat that may be a reservoir for the Ebola virus.

containing a droplet of saliva from the reservoir creature. The chimp becomes sick and dies. A hungry villager, such as the hunter from Gabon, scavenges the dead chimp to feed his family. And with that meal, Ebola spills over to humans.

Nearly two-thirds of all infectious diseases cross from animals to humans, such as malaria, influenza, and rabies. Scientists who study the ecology of West Africa have tested hundreds of species of animals since the first Ebola outbreak in 1976. In early studies, scientists captured and tested bedbugs from Ebola-affected villages, but they did not find any sign of the virus. After outbreaks in the 1990s and the early 2000s, scientists examined blood samples and slices of liver, spleen, and kidney tissue from a wide variety of animals including monkeys, rats, rodents, squirrels, bats, birds, tortoises, snakes, mongooses, and duikers (an African antelope). No Ebola virus was found.

In 2003 a group of disease detectives found evidence of Ebola antibodies in fruit bats. The antibodies suggested that the bats fought off an Ebola infection at one time in their lives. One of these detectives was Dr. Eric Leroy, a veterinarian who also

Eric Leroy, French veterinarian and Ebola virus specialist, works in a laboratory at the International Center for Medical Research in Franceville, Gabon.

specializes in the study of viruses. In 2007 Dr. Leroy linked Ebola to a villager and his daughter who ate a fruit bat. The father survived, but the four-year-old girl died.

Could fruit bats be Ebola's reservoir? Yes, but Dr. Leroy wants to find live Ebola virus in a bat to be sure. Unfortunately, Ebola outbreaks are necessary for him to gather more data and no one can predict where or when an outbreak will occur. "The virus seems to decide for itself," Dr. Leroy said.

From 1976 to 2013, Ebola occurred sporadically in isolated villages. But in 2014, Ebola made headlines. It arrived in busy West African cities with hundreds of thousands of people and grew into the biggest Ebola outbreak the world had ever seen.

Africa's Apes

Human beings and apes suffer from many of the same illnesses, such as colds, tuberculosis, and Ebola. In fact, poaching, habitat destruction, and Ebola virus are the leading threats to Africa's chimpanzees and gorillas. During the 2014 Ebola epidemic, 95 percent of western lowland gorillas that contracted the virus died. Solitary males seem more resistant to the disease than the females and the youngsters that live in groups. Scientists worry that Ebola could put western lowland gorillas near the top of the endangered species list.

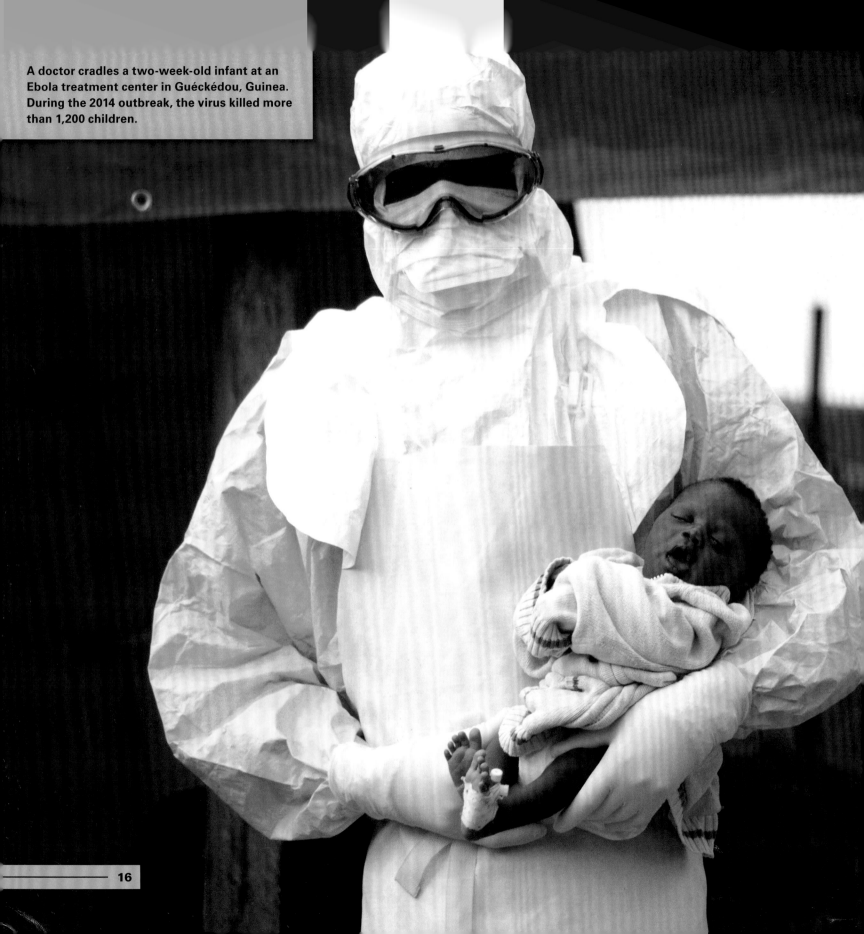

A doctor cradles a two-week-old infant at an Ebola treatment center in Guéckédou, Guinea. During the 2014 outbreak, the virus killed more than 1,200 children.

CHAPTER TWO

THE 2014 HOT ZONE

On December 25, 2013, a two-year-old boy named Emile Ouamouno from the village of Meliandou in southern Guinea developed typical Ebola symptoms: fever, vomiting, and bloody diarrhea. He died on December 28. Emile was Patient Zero in a new Ebola outbreak. His three-year-old sister and his mother died soon after. Three neighbor women washed Mrs. Ouamouno's blood from her house. The three women subsequently became sick and died. A traditional healer conducted a ceremony for sick and healthy people of the village. Hand-holding and even hugs might have spread Ebola to others through the villagers' sweat during this ceremony. When Emile's grandmother fell ill, she left the village to find help. Ebola was on the move.

Guinea, a country in West Africa, had no experience with Ebola. Doctors were caught unprepared because previous outbreaks had been confined to central Africa. Residents of Meliandou didn't know how to prevent the disease from spreading.

They sought help at a clinic in nearby Guéckédou run by Doctors Without Borders, an organization that provides medical care and equipment to troubled countries and to patients in remote areas.

The 2014 Ebola outbreak began with a young boy who lived in Meliandou, Guinea. Before the outbreak, most villagers tended corn, palm, and coffee in their fields.

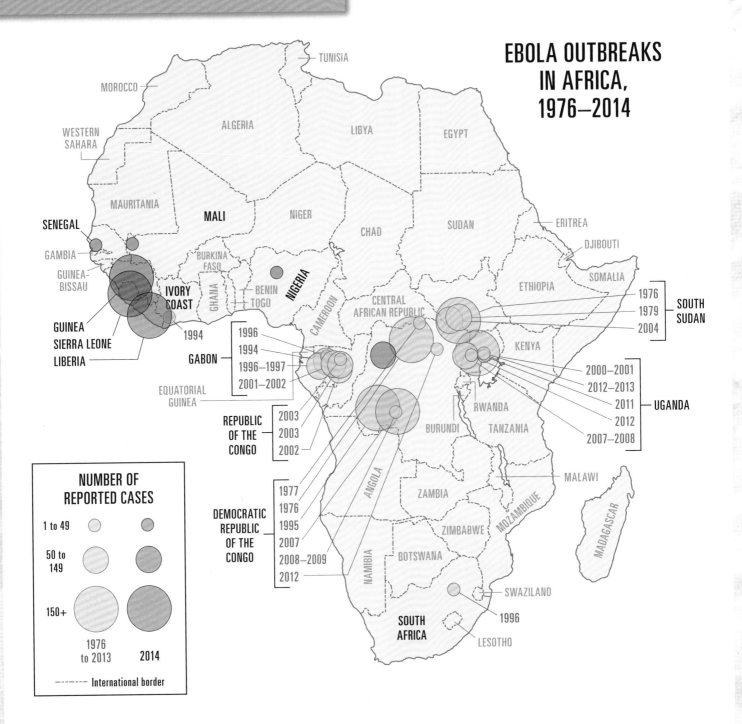

Between 1976 and 2012, the Ebola virus killed about 1,580 people. Nearly seven times that number died in the 2014 epidemic.

EBOLA OUTBREAKS IN AFRICA, 1976–2014

TUNISIA

MOROCCO

WESTERN SAHARA

ALGERIA

LIBYA

EGYPT

MAURITANIA

MALI

NIGER

CHAD

SUDAN

ERITREA

DJIBOUTI

SENEGAL

GAMBIA

GUINEA-BISSAU

BURKINA FASO

NIGERIA

SOMALIA

ETHIOPIA

1976
1979
2004

SOUTH SUDAN

IVORY COAST

GHANA

BENIN
TOGO

CAMEROON

CENTRAL AFRICAN REPUBLIC

KENYA

GUINEA
SIERRA LEONE
LIBERIA

1994

GABON

1996
1994
1996–1997
2001–2002

2000–2001
2012–2013
2011
2012
2007–2008

UGANDA

EQUATORIAL GUINEA

REPUBLIC OF THE CONGO

2003
2003
2002

RWANDA

BURUNDI

TANZANIA

DEMOCRATIC REPUBLIC OF THE CONGO

1977
1976
1995
2007
2008–2009
2012

ANGOLA

MALAWI

ZAMBIA

MOZAMBIQUE

MADAGASCAR

ZIMBABWE

NAMIBIA

BOTSWANA

SWAZILAND

SOUTH AFRICA

1996

LESOTHO

NUMBER OF REPORTED CASES

1 to 49

50 to 149

150+

1976 to 2013   2014

------- International border

Doctors Without Borders began a campaign to educate the Guinean people about Ebola. Doctors, nurses, and volunteers wore protective suits and sprayed chlorine on potentially infected surfaces. The locals were scared, and they blamed visiting health-care workers for spreading the disease. Some villagers chased away the volunteers. A few villagers tried to hide the sick. "You saw the fear in people's faces," said Ella Watson-Stryker, an educator with Doctors Without Borders. "They didn't understand what was going on."

Dr. Joanne Liu, the president of Doctors Without Borders, warned the Guinean government to educate its people and restrict travel to neighboring countries. "We were quickly told . . . that we were crying wolf," Liu said. The government did not want to panic everyone. The sick traveled to the neighboring countries of Sierra Leone and Liberia. Confirmed cases of Ebola reached Liberia at the end of March and Sierra Leone in May. But doctors and nurses worried about the unreported cases. Was Ebola spreading faster than anyone suspected?

Doctors from the Centers for Disease Control and Prevention (CDC) arrived in Guinea in March. The CDC is a US-based organization with more than two thousand

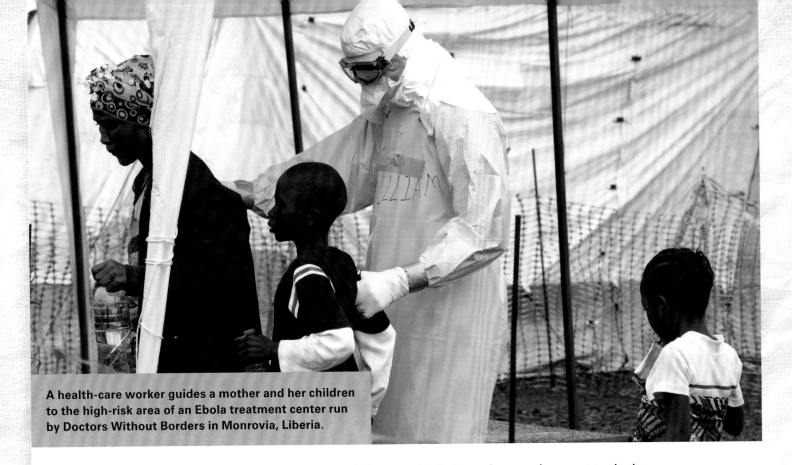

A health-care worker guides a mother and her children to the high-risk area of an Ebola treatment center run by Doctors Without Borders in Monrovia, Liberia.

field-workers in sixty countries around the world. It has the equipment to halt epidemics quickly. However, the World Health Organization (WHO) in Guinea insisted they did not need help. The CDC left and didn't return until August. Unfortunately, WHO underestimated the scope of the Ebola problem.

The health systems of Guinea, Sierra Leone, and Liberia are poor by US standards. They are short on doctors, medical equipment, and medications routinely available in the United States. Like Guinea, these governments failed to respond quickly. If they had, the 2014 Ebola outbreak might never have become an epidemic. By May 30, 2014, 193 people had died. Many more were sick. Hospitals in Guinea, Sierra Leone, and Liberia did not have the beds or the staff to care for them.

Despite the assistance from various international groups, Ebola raged on in West Africa through June. By July 6, the death toll had risen to 518.

Fear contributed to the spread of the virus. Many West Africans did not trust the foreign doctors and nurses in the clinics. They believed that sorcerers cast evil spells to kill people, and these spells could only be reversed by their local medicine man. A few people blamed tourists on safaris for spreading the disease.

In July, Ebola spread to yet another country. Naturalized US citizen Patrick Sawyer traveled to Liberia to care for his sister who ultimately died from the virus. Sawyer then boarded a plane for a conference in Nigeria. He vomited during the flight, when he arrived in Lagos, and again in the car that drove him to the hospital. At first, Sawyer argued he should be released, perhaps because he'd planned to fly home to Minnesota to celebrate his daughters' birthdays in August. Hospital staff refused to release him because they suspected he had Ebola. They were right. Lagos is a huge city with a population of twenty-one million—bigger than Los Angeles and New York City combined. Fortunately, doctors in Nigeria mobilized a network of contact tracers used in the past for outbreaks of polio and lead poisoning. They were able to contain the virus before it infected a large number of people. Only eight Nigerians died of Ebola.

At the end of July, Americans Kent Brantly and Nancy Writebol tested positive for Ebola. They volunteered at an Ebola treatment center in Liberia. Health-care workers

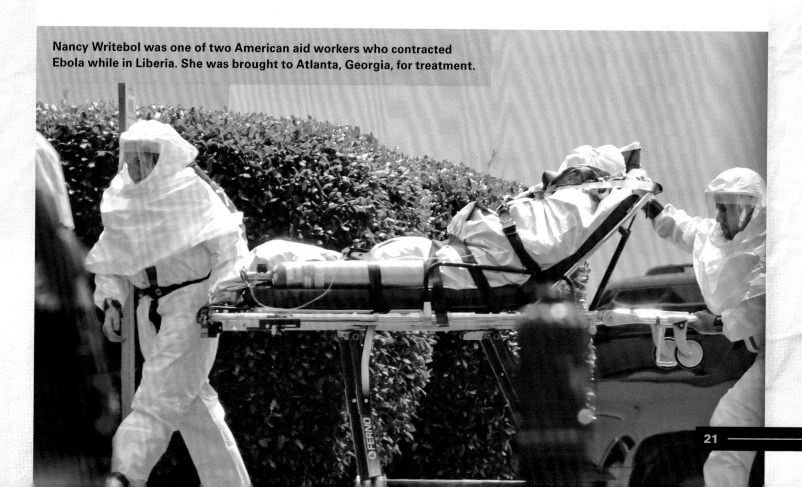

Nancy Writebol was one of two American aid workers who contracted Ebola while in Liberia. She was brought to Atlanta, Georgia, for treatment.

Security forces in Guinea stop travelers at a roadblock where health-care workers take their temperature before clearing them to pass. Thomas Eric Duncan would have passed through similar checkpoints at the Monrovia airport in Liberia.

and volunteers wear gloves, masks, and other protective clothing when they come into contact with Ebola patients. But accidental infections can still occur if even one droplet of fluid containing the virus splashes on their skin or in their eyes when they remove the suits.

Brantly and Writebol received an experimental drug called ZMapp, which had never been tested on humans. They were also flown to Atlanta, Georgia, for treatment. Although Brantly and Writebol both recovered, they proved that the rest of the world was not immune to the virus. US news coverage about Ebola skyrocketed when they became ill. Americans began to worry that the disease could spread to the United States.

In late September 2014, the Ebola virus hopscotched across the Atlantic Ocean inside an international passenger. Thomas Eric Duncan left Monrovia, Liberia, to visit his son in Dallas, Texas. Three separate temperature-screening checkpoints at the Monrovia airport cleared him to fly. His health-screening questionnaire indicated he had not cared for any Ebola patients before leaving Liberia. But that wasn't true. On September 15, he had carried a pregnant friend to an Ebola treatment center. The center turned the woman away because of a shortage of beds. The woman died a few hours later.

On September 25, Duncan went to a Texas hospital with flu-like symptoms similar to the early stages of Ebola. He told a nurse he had traveled from Liberia, but the information never reached the doctors and no one is sure why. Duncan was sent home. Two days later, an ambulance brought Duncan to the same hospital. He was very ill and the fact that he came from Liberia set off warning bells. When Duncan's Ebola test came back positive, health-care workers isolated him so he could not infect other patients. They traced all the people he'd met while in Dallas to see if the infection had spread to them. Duncan died on October 8, the first person ever to die of Ebola in the United States.

Fortunately, none of the people Duncan had contact with before he was hospitalized developed Ebola. However, Amber Jay Vinson and Nina Pham, two nurses who treated Duncan at the Texas hospital, tested positive for the virus. The day before Vinson

Nina Pham *(center)* is one of two nurses who developed Ebola after treating patient Eric Duncan in Dallas, Texas.

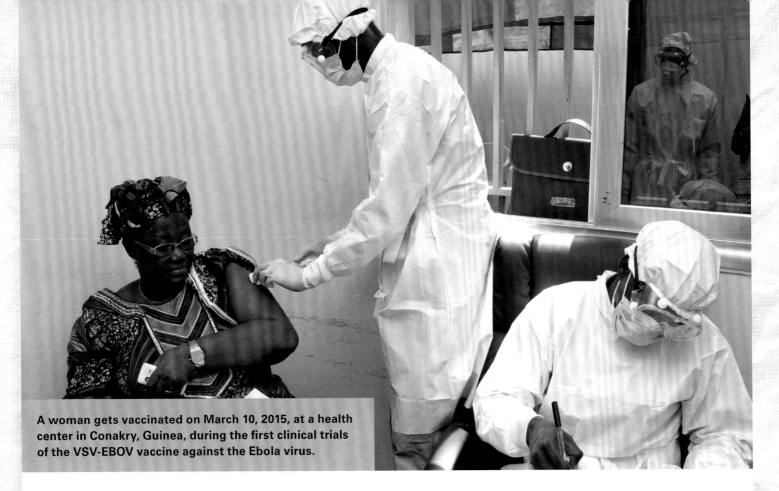

A woman gets vaccinated on March 10, 2015, at a health center in Conakry, Guinea, during the first clinical trials of the VSV-EBOV vaccine against the Ebola virus.

developed symptoms, she boarded an airplane to visit her family in Ohio. Fear fanned by headlines spread more rapidly than the virus. Americans worried that Ebola might have spread to the passengers on Vinson's plane. It had not. Nurses around the country began to worry that their training and their protective gear were inadequate. Two schools in Dallas closed because the mother of two students treated Duncan at the Texas hospital. Two Ohio schools closed because a staff member traveled on Amber Vinson's plane. A cruise ship carrying a Texas health-care worker who might have handled one of Duncan's lab tests was not allowed to dock at its Mexican port.

The CDC had assured Americans it was ready to stop Ebola if it ever reached our shores. But the first hospital to encounter it failed. Duncan was initially sent home, and two of his nurses contracted the virus. Even though the nurses survived, many Americans were scared.

Through the remainder of 2014, the number of new Ebola cases continued to rise in Guinea, Sierra Leone, and Liberia. Mali reported seven confirmed cases. Senegal and

How Ebola Stacks Up

Ebola is not the only virus in recent years to cause fear of a pandemic. SARS (severe acute respiratory syndrome) and HIV (human immunodeficiency virus) triggered the same worry.

Small mammals called Asian palm civets act as the reservoir for SARS. Unlike Ebola, SARS is an airborne virus spread by coughing, sneezing, or even breathing. Scientists say SARS is more contagious than Ebola because, on average, one SARS patient may infect up to four people, while one Ebola patient infects one or two others. Like Ebola, no cure exists for SARS. In 2003 international air travel spread SARS to twenty-nine countries, including the United States. The first patient was a businessman who traveled from China through Hong Kong to Vietnam. Hundreds of people died, including the businessman and the doctor who treated him. Fear spread. Public health officials responded quickly with advanced medical care, and the SARS outbreak ended in about seven months. Nearly 10 percent of SARS patients died. Even though the disease seemed to disappear in 2004, experts believe it could return, and they still consider it extremely dangerous.

African monkeys and chimpanzees are the reservoir for HIV, the virus that causes AIDS. In fact, HIV and Ebola come from the same region in central Africa. The virus first spilled over to humans around 1930 when villagers in Cameroon butchered or ate infected animals. Ebola hits full force, like a freight train rumbling down the

tracks, but HIV stalks quietly like a lion. People may not feel sick enough to visit the doctor for years, yet they are contagious and can pass the virus to others. Most of the world didn't know a pandemic was under way until 1982, when HIV reached five continents.

Similar to people with the Ebola virus, people who develop AIDS from HIV usually die from other infections because their immune systems are too weak to function. Drugs can slow the speed with which the virus replicates, but there is no vaccine and no cure. WHO estimates that 35 million people worldwide live with HIV. In 2013 alone, 2.1 million people were newly infected and more than 1.5 million people died.

Fear of HIV and AIDS swept the world in the 1980s and the 1990s. People with AIDS or who were thought to have HIV were shunned, evicted from their homes, fired from their jobs, and barred from schools. Similar feelings of fear and uncertainty surrounded the 2014 Ebola epidemic.

Spain reported one each. On a more positive note, Nigeria declared itself Ebola-free on October 20, 2014.

At the start of 2015, the Ebola epidemic entered its second year and the number of new cases fell for several weeks in a row. Trials for Ebola vaccines and antiviral medicines began in February in Liberia. But the battle was not yet won. Falling infection rates meant decreased financial support to fight the virus. Doctors Without Borders said that a single new infection could reignite an outbreak. WHO warned that if funding and the supply of volunteer aid workers dried up, it could take another year to halt Ebola. Ominous warnings, yes, but the number of new Ebola cases had risen once again in Guinea and Sierra Leone by early February.

In March a twenty-eight-day stretch without any new Ebola cases came to an end in Monrovia, Liberia. Ruth Tugbah, a street vendor, tested positive for the virus. She shared a one-bathroom house with fifty-two other people and sold food at a school with an enrollment of more than 1,900 students. Health-care workers worried about the number of people she exposed to the virus. And sure enough, a few days after Tugbah tested positive, her eighteen-year-old daughter developed Ebola-like symptoms.

Would the Doctors Without Borders warning become a reality? Would Tugbah be the single patient to ignite a new outbreak?

Liberia has a second chance to practice quick, decisive action to halt Ebola's deadly rampage. Unlike the early days of the 2014 epidemic, an army of volunteers is on hand to trace Tugbah's contacts and hopefully stop the spread of the virus before it blossoms out of control again.

"There is no room for optimism as long as you are dealing with an Ebola virus," said Dr. Bruce Aylward, who leads the WHO response team. "It's not about low numbers. It's about zero. We have got to get to zero."

Putting Ebola in Perspective

Ebola is just one of many viruses that can be transmitted by animal reservoirs. The following table lists the characteristics of a number of viral infections that have affected humans in recent years:

Virus	Animal reservoir	Target	First spillover to humans	Transmission	Classification	Treatment?	Cure?
Ebola	Fruit bats (most likely)	Immune system	1976 Zaire (now Democratic Republic of the Congo)	Contact with bodily fluids	Epidemic 2014	In experimental stages	No
HIV (human immunodeficiency virus)	African monkeys or chimpanzees	immune system	Around 1930	Sexual contact or sharing needles	Pandemic 1980-present	Yes	No
SARS (severe acute respiratory syndrome)	Asian palm civets	Respiratory system	2002 southern China	Airborne	Epidemic 2003-2004	No	No
MERS CoV (Middle East respiratory syndrome)	Camels	Respiratory system	2012 Saudi Arabia	Contact with infected camels; so far, low human to human transmission	Outbreaks	No	No
Common influenza	Pigs infected by wild birds	Respiratory system	Probably 5,000 years ago in central Asia	Airborne	Pandemics 1918-1919 and 2009	Yes	No
Avian influenza	Wild birds	Respiratory system	1997	Handling infected wild birds or poultry; low human-to-human transmission	Outbreaks 1997, 2004	Yes	No
West Nile virus	Birds infected by mosquito bites	Central nervous system	Spread to the United States in 1999	Mosquito bites	Epidemic	No	No
Hantavirus	Rodents or their urine and droppings	Respiratory system	1993 (Sin Nombre strain)	Airborne—stirred up when dried rodent droppings and urine are disturbed	Outbreaks	No	No

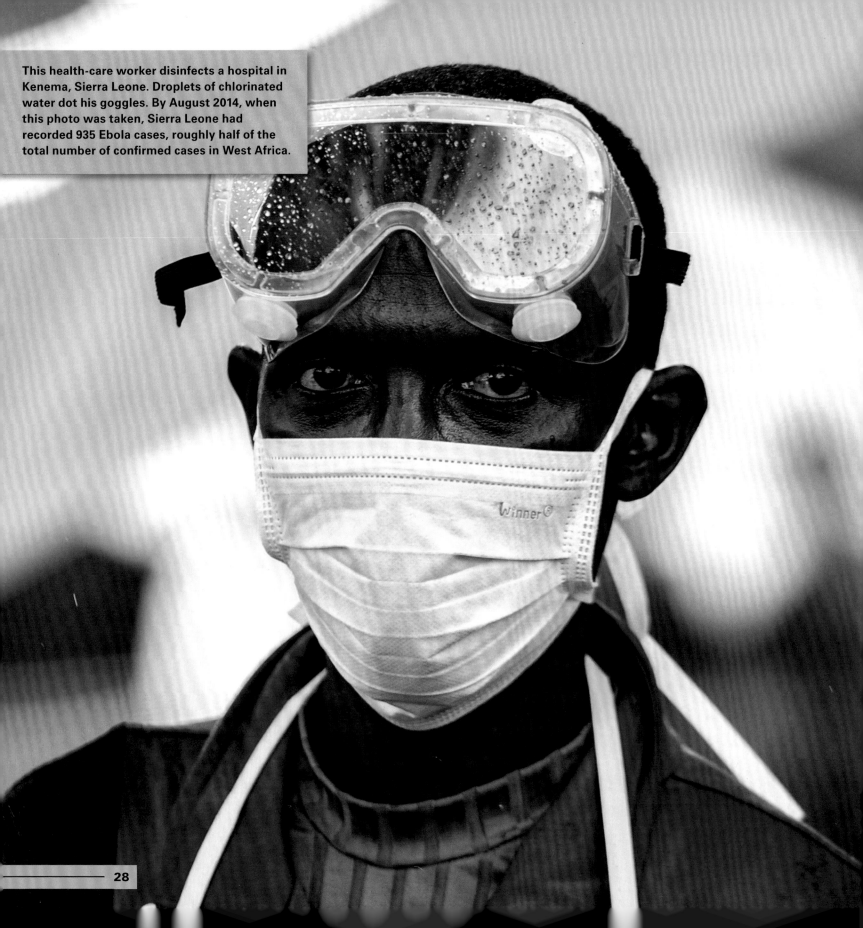

This health-care worker disinfects a hospital in Kenema, Sierra Leone. Droplets of chlorinated water dot his goggles. By August 2014, when this photo was taken, Sierra Leone had recorded 935 Ebola cases, roughly half of the total number of confirmed cases in West Africa.

CHAPTER THREE

ON THE FRONT LINES

What was it really like for the doctors, nurses, volunteers, patients, and scientists who fought Ebola daily during the 2014 outbreak? Many of the frontline workers in the fight against Ebola received low wages or no pay at all. They were ordinary people who set aside their fears and risked their personal safety to help control the crisis. Dr. Jerry Brown converted the chapel on the grounds of his mission in Monrovia, Liberia, into an Ebola isolation unit. Melvin Gibson buried dead Ebola victims—fifty-two on his first day on the job. Foday Gallah drove an ambulance and helped a four-year-old boy with Ebola. Gallah became ill after the boy vomited on him, but both Gallah and the boy survived.

Health-care workers are routinely sprayed with chlorinated water when they enter and exit an Ebola treatment center.

Doctors Without Borders was one of the first organizations to respond to the 2014 outbreak, and its volunteers continue to serve. The hardest-hit areas did not have enough hospitals or clinics to care for patients, so Doctors Without Borders built temporary treatment centers on football-field-sized plots of land carved from the jungle. Doctors, nurses, and local volunteers tested patients, cared for the sick, supervised

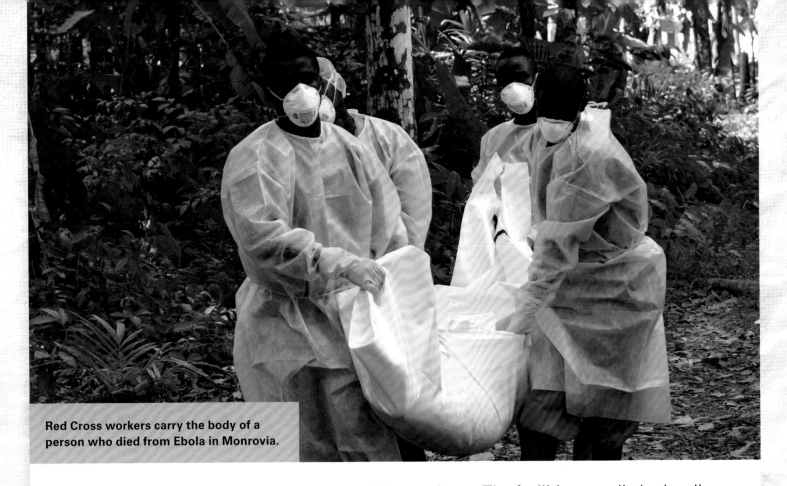

Red Cross workers carry the body of a person who died from Ebola in Monrovia.

the removal of the dead, and celebrated the survivors. The facilities usually had walls of white or blue plastic that cocooned plastic-covered mattresses and equipment for approximately fifty patients. Plastic orange fencing divided the patients who tested positive for Ebola from the patients waiting for test results. Pickup trucks with plastic covers doubled as ambulances. The hum of generators reminded workers that electricity was a luxury not normally available in the jungle.

"It's otherworldly," Dr. Colin Bucks said of his Liberian treatment center. "We're in an area . . . cut out of deep green forest, and everything is blue or gravel, and it smells like chlorine. [It feels as if] you've come to another planet."

In Dr. Bucks's clinic, Liberian volunteers disinfected mattresses, burned patient waste, and buried the dead. They sang hymns before each shift to lift their spirits. "This is our sacrifice," one young man from a burial team said. These local people understood the importance of doing their jobs well. At the treatment center, they were heroes.

Donning and Doffing

Health-care workers must wear protective gear when they care for Ebola patients, including a jumpsuit, an apron, booties to cover shoes, two pairs of gloves, a hood, a face mask, and a face shield. No jewelry or phones are allowed. The gear takes about twenty minutes to don (put on) and about twenty-five minutes to doff (remove). Doctors and nurses attend training classes to learn the correct procedure. The gear must be donned and doffed in a specific order to protect health-care workers from infection. A trained observer monitors each step and checks it off a list. Health-care workers wash their hands—even with gloves on—several times during the process.

Every person who treats Ebola patients or handles their waste must suit up in head-to-toe plastic protective gear. The air of West Africa's tropical climate is hot and heavy with humidity. Everyone sweats a lot. Health-care workers spend only forty-five minutes swathed in protective gear before the heat becomes unbearable. "The tough part is when the masks get filled with your own breath and sweat," Dr. Bucks said. "Then it really gets hard to breathe. You have to get out. You feel like you're suffocating." The hot suits limit the amount of time that doctors, nurses, and volunteers can spend with their patients.

Most Ebola patients isolated in West African treatment centers die a lonely death. To halt the spread of the virus, family members are not allowed to sit around the bedside. Doctors and nurses wrapped like mummies in protective gear often write their names on their hoods so patients can tell them apart. "It's very difficult to interact with people through three pairs of gloves," said Cokie van der Velde, a grandmother from England who volunteers for Doctors Without Borders. "I try to touch people and stroke people because they won't have had any physical contact since they've been in [the treatment center]. When I look in their eyes . . . I see a lot of fear. If they haven't become confused, I quite often see despair."

Thousands of children in West Africa have been orphaned because of Ebola. Four-year-old Sweetie Sweetie's father and sister died from the virus. When her mother began vomiting blood, an ambulance drove them to a treatment center in the town of Port Loko in Sierra Leone. Sweetie Sweetie had nowhere else to go. Health-care workers allowed her to sleep next to her mother in the hospital. Even though Sweetie Sweetie was a young child, she tried to feed her mother and wash her dirty clothes. When her mother died, Sweetie Sweetie's relatives and neighbors refused to take her in because they feared she might spread the virus to them. So she moved to a group home that cares for dozens of Ebola orphans. She asks visitors, "Do you want me?"

Sweetie Sweetie spent more than two weeks at the treatment center, and remained healthy without protective gear. Why didn't she contract Ebola from her family or any

Sometimes Ebola survivors are left without family, such as four-year-old Sweetie Sweetie. Here she sits in her bedroom at the group home in Port Loko, Sierra Leone, where she now lives.

Klubo Mulbah *(center, in blue)* celebrates with friends and family after recovering from Ebola. Mulbah, a health-care worker in Monrovia, Liberia, was infected while caring for a patient.

of the other sick people at the center? Scientists are not yet sure. Perhaps her immune system was able to make enough antibodies to keep her healthy. One thing is clear, though. Scientists need to study survivors like Sweetie Sweetie to see if the secret of their immunity can be shared with others.

Another group of survivors actually became sick with Ebola and recovered. Doctors believe these survivors are immune to Ebola, but they are not certain. "To the best of my knowledge, there has not been a case of a person who has been infected who has recovered and has been infected again," said Marie-Paule Kieny of WHO. Many survivors test their immunity by working as ambulance drivers, gravediggers, or treatment center aids. Amie Subah feeds Ebola patients, gives them medicine, and changes children's diapers. The difference for Subah? She does not have to wear the full protective suit, which allows her to stay with her patients longer. Other survivors help train health-care workers to care for Ebola patients. Only survivors can explain what it was like to have Ebola and what they needed when they were sick.

Unfortunately, Ebola survivors and volunteers in West Africa face stigma and rejection because of the fear that surrounds the virus. Nineteen-year-old Marie Lama said Ebola survivors are treated "like ghosts. People don't want our money or to sell us food. Sometimes I will give the money to friends just so they can go and buy [me] something to eat." Volunteers who return to their villages each day after working with Ebola patients are treated as outcasts. Nelson Sayon worked on a burial team in Liberia collecting still contagious dead bodies. Frightened people threw rocks at his vehicle.

Other frontline workers include scientists who search for the place Ebola hides between outbreaks. A team of thirty disease detectives from Germany, Sweden, and the Ivory Coast in West Africa followed up on Dr. Leroy's work about Ebola's reservoir animal. They believe a tiny insect-eating bat, rather than a large fruit bat, may be responsible for the 2014 epidemic. Such a bat roosted in a hollow tree in which two-year-old Emile played. Guinean children often hunt this bat and grill it like we would toast marshmallows. Does Ebola hide in both insect-eating and fruit-

Liberian burial team members help each other put on protective clothing before retrieving a body of an Ebola victim.

Truth or Hype?

We live in an information age. Television, radio, newspapers, Facebook, Twitter, and word of mouth are just some of the ways we receive news. Some sources provide accurate information. Some do not. Sometimes news spreads so quickly that mistakes creep in. Before they can be corrected, the news is passed on. How do we tell which sources are trustworthy? The next time you come across a story about Ebola—or any other topic—ask yourself the following questions:

1. What does the storyteller want us to remember?
2. How might different people understand the story?
3. Does the storyteller present facts or opinions? How do we know? What words are used? Does the storyteller quote scientific or eyewitness sources?
4. What action does the storyteller want us to take?
5. Do our emotions influence the way we evaluate the story?

eating bats? No one knows for sure. Yet. But if scientists such as Dr. Leroy and his colleagues locate where the virus hides, the information might help reduce the number of future outbreaks.

Ebola wages a war inside its victims' bodies and within the communities it affects. Foday Gallah, Amie Subah, Colin Bucks, and all the other doctors, nurses, and volunteers are the soldiers who battle the virus. They brave unbearable heat, wear uncomfortable protective gear, and work long hours for little or no pay. They sacrifice because they believe in the power of compassion. Their dedication and perseverance will ensure the war is won.

In Conakry, Guinea, health-care workers teach people how to protect themselves from Ebola virus. Previous outbreaks were located in isolated villages, but the 2014 epidemic posed new challenges because many large West African cities were affected.

CHAPTER FOUR

CONQUERING EBOLA

"Mad-Eye" Moody from the Harry Potter series kept wizards on their guard against the evil Lord Voldemort by bellowing, "Constant vigilance!" His words of warning could also be applied to Ebola.

Fear of modern medicine, ignorance of how the disease progresses, and a slow response helped Ebola spread from isolated villages to busy West African cities in 2014. When Ebola reached US soil, Americans finally understood how an outbreak an ocean away could affect them.

While working to contain the outbreak, relief groups such as Doctors Without Borders partnered with public health agencies in Guinea, Sierra Leone, and Liberia to establish safety guidelines. For instance, border guards stopped travelers to measure their temperatures and spray their vehicles with a chlorine solution that killed the Ebola virus in seconds. Guards also sprayed the travelers themselves. Anyone entering or leaving an Ebola treatment center was also sprayed. Workers visited the homes of confirmed Ebola patients to stamp out the spread of the virus. They washed the sick person's possessions with chlorine and burned items

This school in Conakry, Guinea, was closed during the worst of the Ebola epidemic. Children returning in January 2015 had to have their temperature checked before they could enter.

Ebola is a Killer
Lets Prevent it

Don't SHAKE HANDS with PERSONS showing signs of EBOLA

Wash your HANDS regularly with SOAP & CLEAN WATER

Avoid physical CONTACT

Avoid eating BUSH MEAT cook all FOOD very WELL

If you have Fever, Diarrhea and Vomiting with or without Bleeding
GO IMMEDIATELY TO THE NEAREST HEALTH FACILITY

An Ebola information bulletin board in Monrovia, Liberia

that could not be washed, such as mattresses and pillows.

Volunteers on motorbikes tracked down every person who came in contact with an Ebola patient. Each patient's temperature was monitored for twenty-one days. Those who developed symptoms and tested positive for Ebola within that time were treated at clinics. As of March 8, 2015, the CDC listed 14,482 confirmed cases of Ebola. Imagine the long hours and the army of volunteers necessary to trace the complex web of people each sick person met!

Most of West Africa knew nothing of Ebola before the 2014 outbreak. Constant vigilance was the theme of the education campaign in Guinea, Sierra Leone, and Liberia to instruct people how to protect themselves and their families. Billboards, posters, car signs, and even T-shirts offered continual reminders. Wash hands. Don't scavenge dead animals. Don't eat bats. Learn to recognize the symptoms of Ebola. "Ebola is real. Let's fight it together," read one grocery store uniform.

In large cities such as Monrovia, Liberia, bodies were cremated because there was

News from the Front Lines

When this book went to press, the number of Ebola cases in Sierra Leone and Guinea was again increasing. Liberia confirmed its first new patient in twenty-eight days. New vaccines and antiviral drugs were being tested on human volunteers. Breaking news occurred on the front lines on an almost daily basis. To keep up with the latest developments, visit any of the following websites:

- WHO's Ebola page includes stories from the field, who's funding the fight, and current news reports: http://www.who.int/csr/disease/ebola/en/.

- The CDC's Ebola page updates case counts, travel information, and links to partners in the field: http://www.cdc.gov/vhf/ebola/index.html.

- USAid's website includes the latest updates, facts, and stories of survival and compassion: http://www.usaid.gov/ebola/.

- The Doctors Without Borders site has photos, videos, and patient stories: http://www.msf.org/search?keyword=ebola.

no space for the graves and local residents feared that the dead would contaminate their soil. But the cremations caused disagreement among the people of Monrovia because they did not follow traditional burial customs. In outlying areas, public health officials designed burial guidelines that respected Muslim and Christian religious practices and kept the virus from spreading.

While health-care workers fought to contain the virus in West Africa, scientists raced to find other ways to stop the disease. For example, Dr. Gary Kobinger of Canada helped develop ZMapp, the drug given to Americans Kent Brantley and Nancy Writebol. The drug gives the immune system a fighting chance by covering the tiny Velcro-like spikes on the Ebola virus so it cannot attach to human cells. Kobinger tested his drug on monkeys that he infected with Ebola. It saved them all but had never been tested on humans until the Americans received it in July 2014.

Health wasn't the only thing at risk in West Africa. When Ebola struck, many businesses closed, which left people out of work. No work meant no money to buy food. Liberian schools closed to help stop the spread of the disease. Parents worried their children would fall far behind in their studies. Some students delayed their college plans. Some dropped out of school entirely.

Although Ebola didn't affect large numbers of Americans, that doesn't mean Americans should ignore it and expect people in other countries to handle it. Diseases don't care about international borders. Ebola needs only one infected person traveling across the world to jump from one continent to another. In the 2014 outbreak, the United States and other developed countries failed a test of global citizenship. Ebola exposed an indifference to poorer countries where life is harder. Ebola also exposed huge gaps in West Africa's health-care system. The 2014 outbreak might never have reached epidemic proportions if US, European, and African health-care agencies and governments had cooperated earlier. Most of all, Ebola showed the world that

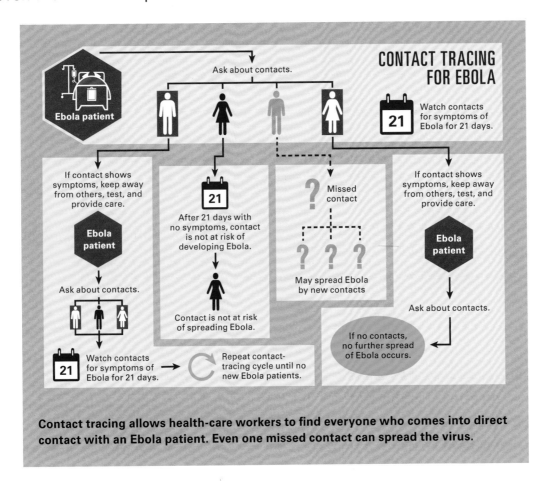

Contact tracing allows health-care workers to find everyone who comes into direct contact with an Ebola patient. Even one missed contact can spread the virus.

education and preparation will be essential to fight the next outbreak. It may not happen for one or three or fifteen years, but it will happen.

Even a small amount of preparation helped Mali, Senegal, and Nigeria halt the spread of the virus. But more is necessary. In January 2015, teams from the CDC, WHO, and other relief organizations assessed the Ebola preparedness of fourteen African nations. Ten out of the fourteen received a rating of less than 28 percent prepared. In response, the relief organizations helped each nation establish Ebola detection and response plans.

"The biggest mistake the world could [make] right now is to blink," said Dr. Aylward of WHO.

As citizens of the world, we are connected to one another. We cannot hide within our borders. To conquer Ebola, or any other disease, we must conquer our fear. Viruses that live inside animal reservoirs, such as Ebola, are nearly impossible to eliminate. But we can fight with the tools at our disposal—cooperative planning, education programs, and new medications to attack the virus before it spreads. Together we can make the world a little bit safer and healthier.

Frequently Asked Questions about Ebola

Q: Is Ebola really killing a lot of people?

A: Yes. Most of these people live in West Africa where there is a shortage of doctors. Many of these people don't go to the hospital until they are very sick. We know that early treatment is a key to helping people survive Ebola. The few people who caught Ebola in the United States received prompt treatment in hospitals.

Q: Can I catch Ebola?

A: Ebola does not spread through the air like the flu virus. It spreads through vomit, urine, feces, saliva, or sweat. You can only get Ebola if you touch the fluids of someone already sick with Ebola and then touch your eyes, mouth, nose, or a cut on your skin.

Q: How do I know if I have Ebola?

A: The symptoms of Ebola are similar to the symptoms of many other viruses: fever, vomiting, diarrhea, muscle aches, and a headache. If you have not been around someone with the Ebola virus, you do not have it. If you feel sick, let a parent or a teacher know. A doctor can help figure out why you're feeling sick.

Q: Why does Ebola kill some people and not others?

A: Some people are lucky to have very strong immune systems that help them fight infections. Others receive early treatment that keeps the virus from growing too strong and allows them to recover.

Q: Is there a vaccine for Ebola?

A: Not yet, but scientists are testing possible vaccines in West Africa.

Q: How do I keep myself healthy?

A: Ebola is very rare in the United States, but it's a good idea to protect yourself from viruses such as the common cold or the flu. Always wash your hands before you touch your mouth, eyes, or nose; before you eat; after you go to the bathroom; and after you touch someone who is sick. Don't touch blood or vomit. Call an adult to clean it up.

Q: Are there rules for washing hands?

A: Use soapy water and sing the "Happy Birthday" song to yourself two times. Be sure to wash in between your fingers and the backs of your hands too.

Q: Will the Ebola epidemic spread to the United States?

A: Possibly. The United States may have more Ebola cases as volunteers return from Sierra Leone, Liberia, and Guinea. But it is unlikely that it will spread in North America the way it has in West Africa. Airports are on alert. US hospitals have special guidelines in place for treating Ebola patients. We have enough beds in isolated units. Health-care workers have been trained to wear protective gear. Be aware of what is happening in the fight against Ebola, but don't worry.

Q: Will Ebola ever become airborne like the flu?

A: Every time a virus such as Ebola infects a new person, it changes a tiny bit. But scientists have never seen a virus spread by fluids change to a virus spread by the air. Ebola lacks the necessary connectors to latch onto our airways and survive. The virus needs a liquid such as blood, saliva, urine, vomit, or sweat to survive.

Schoolchildren in Lagos, Nigeria

In February 2015, I visited a number of schools in Northern California. Several students asked, "What do you want to be when you grow up?" I was flattered they still considered me one of them, but I wasn't sure how to respond. While working on *Ebola: Fears and Facts*, the answer presented itself. I want to be brave and selfless like so many of the Ebola fighters I read about. Their stories touched my heart. I knew I would continue to read and write about them long after this book was completed because they persevered in spite of the odds. And that makes them worth remembering.

Glossary

antibodies: proteins made by the body to defend against viruses and bacteria

chlorine: a greenish-yellow substance with a strong smell commonly used to kill germs in drinking water and swimming pools; it is also found in bleach

contagious: quickly spreading from person to person by contact or closeness

cremate: to burn a dead body to ashes

dehydration: a condition caused by an excessive loss of water

ecology: the study of the way living organisms interact with one another and their environment

electrolytes: substances in body fluid that regulate nerve and muscle function, the body's hydration and pH, blood pressure, and the rebuilding of damaged tissue

epidemic: a disease outbreak that strikes many people in different regions at the same time

hemorrhagic: describing a bloody discharge due to damaged blood vessels

immune: protected against infectious diseases

immune system: a group of organs and cells that defend the body against disease and infection

infectious: capable of being transferred to new individuals

irrigate: to water

naturalize: to allow someone born in another country to become a citizen

Glossary (continued)

organism: a living creature that is dependent on its environment, such as a person, a plant, or an animal

outbreak: a large number of cases of a disease in a short period of time

pandemic: a disease outbreak that spreads around the world

replicate: to copy

reservoir: an organism that stores a virus without any harm to itself

respiratory: relating to the act of breathing

stigma: a set of unfair beliefs that people have about something

Source Notes

2 Karlyn D. Beer, interview with the author, November, 24, 2014.

7 Peter Piot, *No Time to Lose: A Life in Pursuit of Deadly Viruses* (New York: W. W. Norton, 2012), 57.

14 David Quammen, *Ebola: The Natural and Human History of a Deadly Virus* (New York: W.W. Norton, 2014), 72.

19 David von Drehle and Aryn Baker, "2014 Person of the Year: The Ones Who Answered the Call," *Time,* December 22 and 29, 2014, 78.

19 Ibid. 84.

26 Kevin Sack, Sheri Fink, Pam Belluck, and Adam Nossiter, "How Ebola Roared Back," *New York Times*, December 29, 2014, http://www.nytimes.com/2014/12/30/health/how-ebola-roared-back.html.

30 Lara Logan, "The Ebola Hot Zone," transcript, *CBS News*, November 9, 2014, http://www.cbsnews.com/news/the-ebola-hot-zone-liberia/.

30 Beer interview.

31 Logan, "The Ebola Hot Zone."

31 "Surviving Ebola," *NOVA* video, 53:07, October 8, 2014, http://video.pbs.org/video/2365340607/, 7:10.

32 Ibid. 7:15.

32 Jeffrey Gettleman, "An Ebola Orphan's Plea in Africa: 'Do You Want Me?'," *New York Times*, December 13, 2014, http://www.nytimes.com/2014/12/14/world/africa/an-ebola-orphans-plea-in-africa-do-you-want-me.html.

Source Notes (continued)

33 Makiko Kitamura, Simeon Bennett, Michelle Fay Cortez, "Ebola Survivors Become Caregivers, Testing Their Immunity," *Bloomberg Business*, October 21, 2014, http://www.bloomberg.com/news /articles/2014-10-21/ebola-survivors-become-caregivers-testing-their-immunity.

34 Joe Shute, "The Ebola Survivors Saving Lives," *Telegraph* (London). January 9, 2015, http://www .telegraph.co.uk/news/worldnews/ebola/11328607/The-Ebola-survivors saving-lives.html.

37 J. K. Rowling, *Harry Potter and the Goblet of Fire* (New York: Scholastic, 2000), 217.

38 Beer interview.

41 Sheri Fink and Pam Belluck, "One Year Later, Ebola Outbreak Offers Lessons for Next Epidemic," *New York Times*, March 22, 2015, http://www.nytimes.com/2015/03/23/world/one-year-later-ebola -outbreak-offers-lessons-for-next-epidemic.html.

back cover "My Name Is James Harris and I Survived Ebola," YouTube video, 0:55, posted by BBC *Africa*, October 21, 2014, https://www.youtube.com/watch?v=s7WxabqK4js, 0:27.

Selected Bibliography

Beer, Karlyn D, epidemic intelligence service officer at Centers for Disease Control and Prevention. Interview with the author, November 24, 2014.

Logan, Lara. "The Ebola Hot Zone." Transcript. *CBS News*, November 9, 2014. http://www.cbsnews. com/news/the-ebola-hot-zone-liberia/.

"Outbreaks Chronology: Ebola Virus Disease." Centers for Disease Control and Prevention. Accessed November 7, 2014. http://www.cdc.gov/vhf/ebola/outbreaks/history/chronology.html.

Piot, Peter. *No Time to Lose: A Life in Pursuit of Deadly Viruses*. New York: W. W. Norton and Company, 2012.

Quammen, David. *Ebola: The Natural and Human History of a Deadly Virus*. New York: W. W. Norton, 2014.

"Surviving Ebola." *NOVA* video, 53:07. October 8, 2014. http://video.pbs.org/video/2365340607/.

Von Drehle, David, and Aryn Baker. "2014 Person of the Year: The Ones Who Answered the Call." *Time*, December 22 and 29, 2014, 70–107.

Further Reading

Books

Barnard, Bryn. *Outbreak: Plagues That Changed History*. New York: Random House, 2011.

Davies, Nicola. *Tiny Creatures: The World of Microbes*. Cambridge, MA: Candlewick, 2014.

Duke, Shirley Smith. *Infections, Infestations, and Diseases*. Vero Beach, FL: Rourke, 2011.

Koontz, Robin Michal. *The Science of a Pandemic*. Ann Arbor, MI: Cherry Lake, 2015.

Peters, Marilee. *Patient Zero: Solving the Mysteries of Deadly Epidemics*. Toronto: Annick, 2014.

Stewart, Gail B. *SARS*. Farmington Hills, MI: Lucent, 2004.

Wilsdon, Christina, Patricia Daniels, Jen Agresta, and Cynthia Turner. *Ultimate Body-pedia: An Amazing Inside-Out Tour of the Human Body*. Washington, DC: National Geographic Society, 2014.

Websites

BAM! Body and Mind
   http://www.cdc.gov/bam/index.html
   The Centers for Disease Control and Prevention offers information and activities for kids and teachers about diseases, food and nutrition, physical activity, and safety.

"Don't Buy It: Get Media Smart"
   http://pbskids.org/dontbuyit/
   Can you trust the Ebola coverage that you hear on television or read in print? This site from PBS Kids offers tips for thinking critically about media.

MSF Ebola Blog
   http://blogs.msf.org/en/staff/blogs/msf-ebola-blog
   Photos and blog posts from Doctors Without Borders staff describe their experiences during the 2014 Ebola outbreak.

Index

AIDS, 25

bats, 13, 14, 27, 34, 35, 38
burial teams, customs, and
   guidelines, 30, 34, 39

Centers for Disease Control and
   Prevention (CDC), 19–20, 24,
   38, 39

Democratic Republic of the
   Congo, 4, 5, 7, 27
diagram of symptoms, 11, 40
Doctors Without Borders, 17, 19,
   20, 26, 29, 31, 37, 39
Duncan, Thomas Eric, 22–24

Ebola media literacy, 35
Ebola outbreaks, 8–11, 13, 14, 17,
   18; in 1976, 5–7, 13, 18, 27; in
   1996, 9–10, 18; in 2014, 11, 14,
   15, 16, 17–24, 29, 34–35, 37,
   38, 40

education about Ebola, 38, 41

Gabon, 9, 10, 13, 18
Guéckédou, 16–17, 19
Guinea, 16, 17, 18, 19–20, 22, 24,
   26, 34, 36, 37, 38, 39, 43

HIV, 25, 27

Ivory Coast, 18, 34

Liberia, 18, 19, 20, 21, 22, 23, 24,
   26, 29, 30, 33, 34, 37, 38, 39,
   43

Mali, 18, 24, 41
maps, 7, 18

Nigeria, 18, 21, 24, 41

protective clothing and gear, 5, 8,
   10, 19, 21, 29, 31, 34, 35, 43

reservoir species, 12–14, 25, 27,
   34, 41

safety guidelines, 31, 37–38

Senegal, 18, 24, 41
Sierra Leone, 18, 19, 20, 24, 26,
   28, 32, 37, 38, 39, 43
survivors of Ebola, 11, 29–30,
   33–34
symptoms of Ebola, 9, 11, 17, 23,
   42

transmission and spread of
   Ebola, 9–10, 12–13, 17, 20–21,
   22–24, 27, 32–33, 37, 39, 40–41
treatment: chlorine, 19, 29, 37–
   38; drugs, 22, 24, 25, 39, 42;
   hydration, 11, 12; vaccines,
   11, 26, 39; ZMapp, 22, 39

viruses and their characteristics,
   27

World Health Organization
   (WHO), 20, 26, 33, 39

Yambuku, 5–7

Zaire, 5, 7, 8, 10, 27

Photo Acknowledgments

The images in this book are used with the permission of: © iStockphoto.com/Nixxphotography,
pp. 1, 12; © Images of Africa Photobank/Alamy, p. 4; © Peter Piot, p. 5; © Joel Breman, p. 6; © Peter
Hermes Furian/Alamy, p. 7; © Christophe Simon/AFP/Getty Images, p. 8; © Jean-Marc Bouju/AFP/Getty
Images, p. 9; © Malcom Linton/Getty Images, p. 10; © Laura Westlund/Independent Picture Service,
pp. 11, 18, 40; © iStockphoto.com/dangdumrong, p. 13; © Desirey Minkoh/AFP/Getty Images, p. 14;
© iStockphoto.com/powerofforever, p. 15; AP Photo/Kristin Palitza/Picture-Alliance, p. 16; © Jane Hahn/
Washington Post/Getty Images, p. 17; AP Photo/Kristin Palitza/Picture-Alliance, p. 19; © Dominique
Faget/AFP/Getty Images, pp. 20, 38, 41; John Spink/Atlanta Journal-Constitution/MCT/Newscom, p. 21;
AP Photo/Youssouf Bah, pp. 22, 36, 37; AP Photo/The Fort Worth Star-Telegram, Juan Guajardo, p. 23;
© Cellou Binani/AFP/Getty Images, p. 24; AP Photo/Anat Givon, p. 25; © Mohammed Elshamy/Andolu
Agency/Getty Images, p. 28; © Fransico Leong/AFP/Getty Images, p. 29; © Zoom Dosso/AFP/Getty
Images, p. 30; AP Photo/Rex Features, p. 31; © Daniel Berehulak/The New York Times/Redux, p. 32;
© Michel Du Cille/Washington Post/Getty Images, p. 33; © John Moore/Getty Images, p. 34; AP Photo/
Sunday Alabama, p. 43; © R-Studio/Shutterstock.com (paper texture).

Front cover: © John Moore/Getty Images (portraits); © iStockphoto.com/Nixxphotography (virus).